THE CHURCH

LIFE IN VICTORIAN ENGLAND

THE CHURCH

VIRGINIA SCHOMP

MARSHALL CAVENDISH • BENCHMARK
NEW YORK

For MFN Kristyn Schomp

The author and publishers would like to thank Walter L. Arnstein, Professor of History Emeritus at the University of Illinois at Urbana-Champaign, for his valuable comments and careful reading of the manuscript.

Other Marshall Cavendish Offices: Marshall Cavendish International (Asia) Private Limited, 1 New Industrial Road, Singapore 536196 • Marshall Cavendish International (Thailand) Co Ltd. 253 Asoke, 12th Flr, Sukhumvit 21 Road, Klongtoey Nua, Wattana, Bangkok 10110, Thailand • Marshall Cavendish (Malaysia) Sdn Bhd, Times Subang, Lot 46, Subang Hi-Tech Industrial Park, Batu Tiga, 40000 Shah Alam, Selangor Darul Ehsan, Malaysia

Marshall Cavendish is a trademark of Times Publishing Limited
All websites were available and accurate when this book was sent to press.

LIBRARY OF CONGRESS CATALOGING-IN-PUBLICATION DATA Schomp, Virginia. The church / Virginia Schomp. p. cm. — (Life in Victorian England) Includes bibliographical references and index. Summary: "Describes the role of religion in the lives of Victorians, including how it influenced the way they lived, how they observed special occasions, and how they coped with the many changes and challenges of their times"—Provided by publisher. ISBN 978-1-60870-031-8 1. England—Religious life and customs—Juvenile literature. 2. England—Church history—19th century—Juvenile literature. 3. Church of England—History—19th century—Juvenile literature. I. Title. BR759.S347 2010 274.2'081—dc22 2010006901

EDITOR: Joyce Stanton PUBLISHER: Michelle Bisson ART DIRECTOR: Anahid Hamparian SERIES DESIGNER: Michael Nelson

Images provided by Rose Corbett Gordon, Art Editor of Mystic CT, from the following sources: Cover: Mary Evans Picture Library/The Image Works Back cover: Private Collection/Bridgeman Art Library Page 1, 16: Private Collection/Photo Bonhams, London/Bridgeman Art Library; pages 2-3: The Art Archive/Victoria and Albert Museum London/Sally Chappell; page 7: Russell-Cotes Art Gallery and Museum, Bournemouth, UK/Bridgeman Art Library; page 8: Manchester Art Gallery, UK/Bridgeman Art Library; page 11: Fine Art Photographic Library/Corbis; pages 12, 13: Getty Images; page 18: Guildhall Library, City of London/Bridgeman Art Library; page 21: City of London/HIP/The Image Works; pages 22, 70: Private Collection/Photo Christies Images/Bridgeman Art Library; pages 24, 50: Victoria & Albert Museum/Art Resource, NY; pages 25: Yale Center for British Art, Paul Mellon Collection/Bridgeman Art Library; pages 26, 31, 41, 42, 61: Private Collection/Bridgeman Art Library; page 28: Private Collection/Mallett Gallery, London/Bridgeman Art Library; pages 29, 46: Private Collection/The Stapleton Collection/Bridgeman Art Library; page 34: Coram in the care of the Foundling Museum/Bridgeman Art Library; page 36: Graham Reed Fine Art, York, North Yorkshire/Bridgeman Art Library; page 39: Warrington Museum and Art Gallery, Cheshire, UK/Bridgeman Art Library; page 44: The Print Collector/HIP/The Image Works; page 49: Private Collection/Bourne Gallery, Reigate, Surrey/Bridgeman Art Library; page 51: Ann Ronan Picture Library/HIP/Art Resource, NY; page 54: Fine Art Photographic Library, London/Art Resource, NY; page 56: The Art Archive/Bradford City Art Gallery/Eileen Tweedy; page 58: Roy Miles Fine Paintings/Bridgeman Art Library; page 62: Private Collection/Photo Peter Nahum at The Leicester Galleries/Bridgeman Art Library; page 63: National Museum of Photography, Film and Television/SSPL/The Image Works; page 64: Adoc-photos/Art Resource, NY; page 67: Royal Institution/SSPL/The Image Works; page 69: Ullstein - Olaf Rahardt/The Image Works.

Printed in Malaysia (T)
135642

Front cover: Truro Cathedral in the county of Cornwall, England
Half-title page: A young worshiper places a coin in a church collection box.
Title page: A village choir in mid-nineteenth-century England
Back cover: *Florence Cope Saying Grace at Dinnertime* was painted by the girl's artist-father, Charles West Cope.

CONTENTS

ABOUT VICTORIAN ENGLAND

On June 20, 1837, King William IV of England died, and his eighteen-year-old niece, Victoria, ascended the throne. The teenage queen recorded her thoughts in her diary:

> Since it has pleased Providence to place me in this station, I shall do my utmost to fulfil my duty towards my country; I am very young and perhaps in many, though not in all things, inexperienced, but I am sure, that very few have more real good will and more real desire to do what is fit and right than I have.

That blend of religious faith, confidence, devotion to duty, and the earnest desire to do good would guide Victoria through the next sixty-three years and seven months, the longest reign of any English monarch. The queen's personal qualities would also set the tone for the period that bears her name, the Victorian Age.

Today the term *Victorian* is sometimes used to describe someone who is prim and prudish. We may think of Queen Victoria as a stuffy old lady presiding over a long, formal dinner party where everyone watches their language and worries about which fork to use. That image is not entirely wrong. Victoria and her subjects *did* believe in "traditional values" such as duty, discipline, and self-control. Their society *was* governed by a set of strict moral and social rules. However, that is not the whole picture. When we look deeper, we discover that the Victorian era, far from being dull and predictable, was a period of extraordinary change. Between 1837 and 1901, England was transformed from a mostly agricultural, isolated society into a modern industrial nation with territories all over the world. The Victorian people witnessed astonishing advances in science and technology, as well as sweeping political, legal, and social reforms. A Victorian physician named Sir Henry Holland described his exciting times as "an age of transition, a period when changes, deeply and permanently affecting the whole condition of mankind, are occurring more rapidly, as well as extensively, than at any prior time in human history."

Life in Victorian England takes a look at this dynamic era, with a focus on the people and their everyday lives. The four books in the series will introduce us to men, women, and children at all levels of society, from poor farmers and factory workers to striving middle-class families to the aristocrats at the top of the social scale. In this volume we will meet the priests, ministers, and other religious leaders of Victorian England. We will see how religion influenced the way the Victorians lived, how they observed special occasions, and how they coped with the many changes and challenges of their times.

Now it is time to step back to a world that is poised on the brink of the modern age. Welcome to an era when gas lamps are giving way to electric lightbulbs, stagecoaches to locomotives, wooden sailing vessels to iron warships. Welcome to life in Victorian England!

Above: *Reading the Bible* by the Victorian artist Thomas McEwan

Proud parents show off their newly baptized baby outside a parish church in southern England.

ONE

A CHRISTIAN NATION

Religious life in our great cities takes more varied forms than most people are aware of. Not even the divergent types of the Anglican church . . . can satisfy the restless individuality of the human soul.

⁓THE REVEREND BROOKE HERFORD (1867)

VICTORIAN ENGLAND WAS A DEEPLY RELIGIOUS PLACE. The majority of Victorians were raised in Christian households, and the stories, sacraments, and moral teachings of the church were part of their day-to-day lives. Religion offered comfort and stability in tumultuous times. It was a driving force behind the many charitable works and social reforms of the Victorian era. It was also a source of fierce controversy. Throughout the nineteenth century, England's established (or official) church wrestled with conflicts within its own ranks as well as challenges from outside religious bodies. At the same time, the leaders of all the churches struggled to serve the needs of a soaring population in a rapidly changing society.

A NATIONAL CHURCH

Before the reign of King Henry VIII, England was a Catholic nation. In the 1530s Henry decided to divorce his first wife and remarry. The pope, head of the Catholic Church in Rome, refused to grant the divorce. Henry rejected the pope's authority and declared *himself* the supreme head of the church within his dominions. His actions led to the formation of the independent Anglican Church, or Church of England.

The creation of the Church of England was part of a broader religious revolution known as the Protestant Reformation. During this sixteenth-century European movement, a number of protesters, or "protestants," separated from the Catholic Church and established their own churches. After England's break with Rome, the Anglican Church gradually combined its Catholic roots with beliefs and practices borrowed from the other Protestant churches. By Victorian times, England's established church had assumed the basic form in which it would continue to the present day.

The Church of England was (and is) organized much like the Catholic Church. The smallest unit is the local parish, headed by a parish priest. Several parishes together make up a deanery, administered by a priest called a dean. A group of deaneries is an archdeaconry, under an archdeacon. Archdeaconries are grouped into dioceses, under the authority of a bishop. An archbishop presides over a province, or large group of dioceses. There are two archbishops in the Church of England, the archbishops of Canterbury and York.

All the members of this complex organizational structure swear an oath of loyalty to the "supreme governor" of the church, the reigning king or queen. This is just one of the many signs of the close relationship between church and state in England. As the nation's established church, the Church of England enjoys special legal and

legislative privileges, including seats for twenty-six senior bishops in Parliament's House of Lords. Appointments of high-ranking clergy must be approved by the monarch, in consultation with the prime minister. Queen Victoria took an especially serious view of this responsibility. She viewed the selection of bishops as a matter of "immense importance" and "great anxiety. . . . The men to be chosen must not be taken with reference to satisfying one or the other party in the Church, or with reference to any political party—but for their real worth."

The graceful steeple of a parish church towers over a Victorian village.

HIGH, LOW, AND BROAD

All Anglicans share certain basic beliefs and practices. They believe that the Bible is the revealed word of God, containing the core of all Christian thought. They celebrate two sacraments borrowed from the Catholic Church: baptism and Holy Communion. Their worship services are based on the Book of Common Prayer, a collection of readings, psalms, prayers, and devotions first published in 1549, soon after the church's break with Rome. The Book of Common Prayer includes the Thirty-nine Articles of Religion, a formal statement of beliefs issued in 1563 to define the Church of England and set it apart from the Catholic Church.

Along with these broad areas of agreement, there were sharp divisions within the Anglican community from the moment the church was formed. In the years leading up to the Victorian period, the conflicts intensified as church members proposed different ways of responding to the changes taking place in English society. By the time Victoria took the throne, three major factions had emerged within the Church of England: High Church, Low Church, and Broad Church.

A priest dressed in rich vestments baptizes a newborn in an Anglo-Catholic church.

The High Church faction stressed the importance of the church's spiritual roots. Its followers, sometimes called Anglo-Catholics, urged a return to the forms and ceremonies of earlier centuries. High Church worship services looked much like those in a Catholic church. The priests dressed in richly embroidered robes, similar to Roman Catholic vestments. They conducted elaborate rituals at altars wreathed in clouds of incense and decorated with golden crosses, candlesticks, flowers, and other ornaments. For some worshipers, the beautiful, mystical setting contributed to a spiritually uplifting experience. Others denounced the Anglo-Catholics' "Popish" practices. One ardent critic described a High Church service as "such a scene of theatrical gymnastics, of singing, screaming, genuflections [bending the knee], and a series of strange movements of the priests . . . as I never saw before even in a Romish Temple."

Low Church services were far less elaborate. Priests belonging to the Low Church, or Evangelical, faction of the Anglican Church dressed in plain black robes and performed their simple rituals before sparsely decorated altars. Rejecting the Anglo-Catholic emphasis on priestly authority and ritual, Evangelicals embraced the Protestant side of their faith, which stressed the importance of a personal relationship with God and his Son, Jesus Christ. According to Evangelical beliefs, all people are sinners, tainted by the "original sin" of Adam and Eve, who fell from grace in the Garden of Eden. To achieve salvation, the faithful must repent their sins and accept Christ as their personal savior. Evangelicals believe that they are called to carry the Gospel ("good news") of salvation to others, through both words and good works. Their commitment to spreading the Gospel inspired many of the nineteenth century's most notable social reforms, including movements to abolish slavery and improve conditions in city slums and factories.

An Evangelical minister and his congregation celebrate the sacrament of Holy Communion.

The Broad Church fell somewhere in between the High and Low Church factions. Members of this liberal-minded group wanted to ensure that the Church of England remained a vital force in the nation. They believed that the church must be tolerant of different points of view, in order to attract the largest number of followers. Broad Churchmen tended to be committed to social reform and open to new ideas and scientific discoveries. While their faction remained small and loosely organized through most of the Victorian period, Broad Church views would gain widespread acceptance by the early twentieth century.

OUTSIDE THE FOLD

On a Sunday in March 1851, an ambitious survey took a look at the state of religion in England and Wales. Census takers stationed throughout the cities and countryside counted the number of people who attended religious services. The results of the Census of Religious Worship horrified middle-class Victorians who regarded themselves as pillars of a righteous Anglican nation. Less than half the population—7.26 million people out of a total of nearly 18 million—had attended any service at all. Of those who did attend, slightly more than half had chosen *not* an Anglican house of worship but a Nonconformist chapel or Catholic church.

Nonconformists (also called Dissenters) were Protestants who did not conform to the teachings and practices of the Anglican Church. Some of the most prominent Nonconformist sects in England were the Congregationalists, Baptists, Presbyterians, Unitarians, Quakers, and Methodists (including two major branches, the Primitive Methodists and Wesleyan Methodists). While each of these churches had its own teachings, most Nonconformists shared certain basic characteristics. They condemned the privileged status of the established church. Their organizational structure was generally less elaborate and their services less formal than those of the Church of England. The majority of Nonconformists were Evangelicals who, like the Anglican Evangelicals, believed in the divine authority of the Bible and the importance of the individual's personal relationship with God and Christ.

While the Protestant faiths—including both Anglicans and Nonconformists—dominated in Victorian England, the religious census showed that 3.5 percent of the population attended Catholic churches. That figure included hundreds of thousands of immigrants who had fled mostly Catholic Ireland between 1847 and 1850, during the Great Irish Famine. The census necessarily ignored the only other faith with significant representation in England—the small Jewish population, who observed the Sabbath not on Sunday but on Saturday.

A much larger group also had no place in the survey: the millions of Christians who did not regularly attend either church or chapel. An analysis of census results showed that upper- and middle-class Victorians were most likely to attend religious services. Least likely were members of the growing urban working class. One tongue-in-cheek account of working-class life admitted that there were some men who "rise as early on Sunday mornings as they do on other mornings, but such men are regarded as men of evil conscience or bad digestion."

Many hardworking country people also skipped church. Flora Thompson, who grew up in southeast England, observed that "nine out of ten" people in her small village called themselves Anglicans, but

> few went to church between the baptisms of their offspring. . . . About a dozen of their elders attended regularly; the rest stayed at home, the women cooking and nursing, and the men . . . eating, sleeping, reading the newspaper, and strolling round to see how their neighbours' pigs and gardens were looking.

Throughout the Victorian period, clergymen of all denominations would work hard to encourage greater religious devotion among the working classes. At the same time, members of all the parties within and outside the Church of England would continue to debate their differing views of Christianity. All these struggles would make religion a powerful force in Victorian life.

DISPUTES AND DISCRIMINATION

Before 1828 Nonconformist Protestants could not serve in local or national government. Until 1871 only practicing members of the Church of England could study at Oxford or Cambridge, England's most prestigious universities. In the course of the nineteenth century, these and other discriminatory measures against non-Anglicans were gradually overturned. However, bitter rivalries could still erupt between Anglicans and Nonconformists, or what the Victorians called "church and chapel." The gulf between church and chapel was especially wide in the countryside, where most squires and large farmers were Anglican, while laborers tended to align with Dissenting churches.

Above: Jewish scholars study a religious text. England's Jewish population faced prejudice and discrimination during much of the Victorian period.

In the cities disputes between Protestants and Catholics were more common. Many middle-class Victorians regarded the poor Irish Catholic immigrants who settled in city slums as ignorant and vulgar. Evangelical Protestants looked with horror on all Catholics, rich and poor. Edmund Gosse, who grew up in a strict Evangelical household, was taught to loathe "the so-called Church of Rome." As a young boy, Edmund had not yet "formed any idea whatever of the character or pretensions or practices of the Catholic Church, or indeed of what it consisted, or its nature; but I regarded it with a vague terror as a wild beast."

England's Jewish community numbered only about 30,000 at the start of the Victorian Age. Beginning in the 1880s, the numbers swelled as some 100,000 Jewish immigrants fled persecution in eastern Europe to settle in London and other English cities. Many of the immigrants built successful business careers. Prosperous Jews put up handsome synagogues and operated a large number of free schools, hospitals, and other charities. Despite their accomplishments, England's Jews were regarded as outsiders in a Christian nation. The Jewish banker and politician Lionel Rothschild was elected to the House of Commons five times, but he was denied his seat because he refused to take the oath of office "on the true faith of a Christian." A prominent member of the House of Lords argued that Jews were the "degenerate children" of "fallen fathers," who should not serve in Parliament until they became a "people of God [by] being converted to the faith of Christ." Despite such objections, the House of Commons finally voted to admit Jewish members. In 1858 Rothschild took his seat. A quarter century later, his son, Baron Nathaniel Rothschild, became the first practicing Jew in the House of Lords.

St. Giles's Cripplegate in London was one of many older Anglican churches restored during the reign of Queen Victoria.

TWO

STONE CHURCHES *and* SOARING CATHEDRALS

I went into the churchyard under the feathering larch which sweeps over the gate. The ivy-grown old church with its noble tower stood beautiful and silent among the elms with its graves at its feet.
∾THE REVEREND FRANCIS KILVERT, MAY 7, 1871

ONE OF THE GOALS OF THE 1851 RELIGIOUS CENSUS WAS to determine whether there was enough room in the houses of worship in England and Wales to meet the needs of the population. The answer, according to a widely read report on the survey, was no. Horace Mann, the young lawyer given the task of analyzing the returns, found that there were nearly 35,000 churches and chapels, with enough "sittings" for about 8.7 million people—just 49 percent of the population. The shortage was most acute in the areas where the population was growing most rapidly. To make room for everyone, the various Christian denominations would have to build at least 2,000 new churches and chapels. "These sittings, too, must be provided *where* they are wanted [needed most]," Mann urged, "in the *large town districts* of the country."

AN ERA OF CHURCH BUILDING

Even before the 1851 survey, church leaders knew they had a problem. As the Industrial Revolution took root in Great Britain, the population of many small towns and cities exploded. Small parishes designed to serve a few hundred people suddenly found themselves overwhelmed by tens of thousands. The bulk of the population was made up of working-class people who flocked to urban areas to work in the mills and factories. There was not enough room for all these people in the old parish churches, and no way for clergymen to meet the pressing needs of the masses herded into the filthy, overcrowded city slums.

The Anglican Church responded to the challenge by pouring money into church building. In the first half of the nineteenth century, Parliament granted 1.5 million pounds to the newly formed Church Building Society, while more than 10 million pounds was contributed by private donors. The funds were used to build or restore nearly 3,000 places of worship. Members of Nonconformist churches also gave generously to their own building programs, adding nearly 17,000 chapels.

These impressive efforts were not enough to keep pace with the soaring urban population. By midcentury, the Church of England had increased its sittings by 24 percent, but the population had grown by more than 100 percent in the same period. "Whereas in 1801," wrote Horace Mann, "she [the church] supplied accommo-

A well-attended church service in southeast London, 1809. The pews would become ever-more crowded as the city's population soared.

dation for very nearly half the people . . . , she now contributes less than a third."

Mann's report sparked a new round of building. By the end of the century, tens of thousands of churches and chapels had been built or restored. This achievement was funded largely by contributions from men and women of all classes and religious denominations. The donations were inspired by the Victorians' well-developed sense of "Christian duty." They were also fueled, at least in part, by the spirit of competition among Anglicans and Nonconformists. In its 1881 yearbook, the Congregational Church reported that it had added a number of new chapels in the county of Lancashire, center of the cotton industry. The rate of increase, Congregational leaders could not resist pointing out, was far greater than that of the rival Church of England.

PLUSH PEWS AND "RAGGED CHURCHES"

Horace Mann knew that new buildings were only one part of the solution to the problem of declining church attendance. In his report on the 1851 religious census, Mann pointed out one of the chief reasons behind the working classes' growing dislike for organized religion: the pew system. Much of the income in churches came from the rental fees that upper- and middle-class people paid to have their own private pews. These superior sittings at the front of the church often had carpets, seat cushions, and other comforts. Meanwhile, less well-off worshipers sat in the bare, backless "free sittings" at the sides or rear of the building. As this excerpt from Mann's report explains, the segregated seating made poor and working-class people feel unwelcome in church. During the Victorian Age, both the Anglican and Nonconformist churches tried various strategies to remedy the situation, including reducing or eliminating pew rents and offering separate services or even separate churches (sometimes known as "ragged churches") for the working classes.

One chief cause of the dislike which the labouring population entertain for religious services is thought to be the maintenance of those distinctions by which they are separated as a class from the class above them. Working men . . . cannot enter our religious structures without having pressed upon their notice some memento of inferiority. The existence of pews and the position of the free seats are, it is said, alone sufficient to deter them from our churches; and religion has thus come to be regarded as a purely middle-class propriety [special characteristic] or luxury. It is therefore, by some, proposed to abandon altogether the pew system, and to raise by voluntary contributions the amount now paid as seat rents. . . . Other minds [suggest] a different remedy. . . . The labouring myriads [masses], it is argued, forming to themselves a world apart, have no desire to mingle . . . with persons of a higher grade. . . . It has consequently been proposed to . . . strive to get [working-class people] gradually to establish places for themselves. Experiments have been already put in operation with the persons lowest in the social scale; and ragged churches are in several places making a successful start.

Above: A young worshiper occupies one of the "better" pews reserved for more prosperous parishioners.

"CHRISTIAN ARCHITECTURE"

The parish church was a familiar sight across the Victorian countryside. Reflecting some 1,300 years of English history, it came in all sizes, ages, and architectural styles. A few simple stone churches dated all the way back to the seventh century, when Christianity first came to England. Churches from later periods were built in styles including Romanesque, noted for its large towers and rounded arches, and Gothic, with pointed arches and soaring spires. By the early nineteenth century, the most popular church-building style was neoclassical, inspired by the temples of ancient Greece and Rome.

The Victorian Age brought renewed enthusiasm for the Gothic style of the Middle Ages. Followers of the High Church faction of the Church of England embraced this "Gothic Revival." In their view the thirteenth and fourteenth centuries had been a time of exceptional religious devotion, when holy men created the only true "Christian architecture." Most of the new churches built in England's cities after the mid-nineteenth century followed the Gothic Revival style. This romanticized version of Gothic architecture featured pointed arches, steep gables, towers, battlements, and ever-more elaborate decorative touches.

The most magnificent churches were the cathedrals. Each of the Anglican dioceses had its own cathedral, which served as both a house of worship and the "seat," or headquarters, of the bishop. During the Victorian period, several ancient cathedrals were "restored" in line with the Gothic Revival ideals (even if that sometimes meant destroying genuine Gothic features). A handful of old parish churches were restored and raised to cathedral status as new dioceses were formed to serve the growing population. In the 1880s, the Church of England also began the building of one entirely new cathedral, Truro, in southern England.

But it was the Catholic Church that erected the most magnificent new cathedral of the Victorian era. Westminster Cathedral in London, built between 1895 and 1903, pointedly ignored the Gothic Revival style. Built in the Byzantine style of the late Roman Empire, this spectacular brick-and-stone church was an emphatic reminder of the Catholic presence in the midst of a Protestant nation.

INSIDE NAVE AND CHANCEL

The inside of a Gothic Revival church was as impressive as the exterior. Colorful stained glass windows depicted scenes from the Bible and the lives of saints and prophets. Intricately patterned tiles decorated the walls and floors. Ornate wood or iron screens separated an elevated chancel (the area around the altar) from the nave (the main part of the church). A richly carved altar was raised on further steps and placed at the most remote end of the chancel. The chancel also made room for two Victorian-era additions: an organ and a robed choir, inspired by the monks who sang in medieval churches. Every piece of furniture in the church was laid out according to a strict plan designed to fit the elaborate Anglo-Catholic service and encourage spiritual devotion.

Victoria was crowned in London's Westminster Abbey, a glorious Gothic church whose oldest parts date back to the eleventh century.

The new principles of church design gradually found their way into buildings erected by all factions within the Anglican Church, not just the Anglo-Catholic. Where there were no funds for a new building, older churches were often renovated to reflect the more ornate style. Raised chancels were added, along with stalls for the new church choirs. Decorative tiles covered old stone floors. Carved altars covered with rich crimson altar cloths took the place of plain tables and linen cloths. Flora Thompson described the church in her small, remote hamlet as "a tiny place," with "grey, roughcast walls, plain-glass windows, and flagstone floor." Yet even this humble village church boasted a "stained glass window over the altar, glowing jewel-like amidst the cold greyness."

A gentleman-priest preaches from the pulpit of a Victorian church

THREE

THE MEN of the CHURCHES AND CHAPELS

Usually the [Anglican] clergyman is a gentleman by birth,
very likely a relative of the squire's, . . . and by birth, education,
and tradition shares the sympathies of "society". The dissenter
generally has come from a family lower in the social scale.

∾ PETER ANDERSON GRAHAM, *THE RURAL EXODUS* (1892)

NO MATTER HOW MANY CHURCHES AND CHAPELS WERE built, they were not much use without clergy. The 1851 religious census found that England and Wales had fewer than 25,000 Christian clergymen, serving a population of nearly 18 million. The various churches responded to the shortage by expanding their efforts to train and install new priests and ministers. By 1901, there were about 40,000 clergymen, an increase of more than 60 percent.

The new arrivals entered the ministry at a challenging time. The Anglican Church was still a powerful institution, but the many changes percolating through the cities and countryside threatened its traditional role in English life. The Nonconformist sects were gaining in influence, but they struggled to keep pace with the expanding urban society. It would take a new type of clergyman to meet the demands of the age and bridge the growing gap between organized religion and the working classes.

PRIESTLY PRACTICES

In the Church of England, only men who were ordained, or received the sacrament of Holy Orders, were authorized to minister to

Many Anglican priests were educated at the prestigious University of Cambridge.

the public in the name of the church. There were three orders of clergy: bishops, priests, and deacons. Bishops governed the dioceses, and they had the power to ordain new priests and confirm the faithful into the church. Priests were in charge of the parishes. Deacons assisted the parish priests in conducting worship services and ministering to the needy.

The majority of Anglican priests graduated from Oxford or Cambridge. They might earn their degrees in any course of study, not necessarily religion. Young squires and aristocrats often took Holy Orders not because they felt a religious calling but because the church was one of the few respectable fields of employment for a gentleman.

A parish priest's post was called a "living." This was because the priest made his living from the tithe—the annual tax that every parish was required to pay to maintain the local church and its clergyman. Depending on how the tithe was distributed, the priest might be known as a rector (a priest who was entitled to all of the tithe) or a vicar (who received only part). A rector or vicar also might earn income from the lands that came along with his house, the parsonage. The income from livings varied according to the size and wealth of the parish. Some priests barely scraped by, while others lived quite comfortably. Most lived on somewhat less than four hundred pounds a year, a sufficient but not lavish income.

To make ends meet—or add to their existing wealth—many priests held more than one living, a practice called pluralism. A vicar or rector who was responsible for a parish but did not live there usually hired a curate to perform his day-to-day duties. The curate was a fully ordained priest without a living of his own. He worked hard for a very small income, while the priest who paid his salary might do little more than stop by the church to deliver the Sunday sermon. Many Anglicans believed that the widespread neglect of parishes was one of the reasons behind the rise of the Nonconformist churches. A year after Victoria took the throne, Parliament passed a law officially abolishing the practice of pluralism.

The nineteenth century also brought increasing criticism of a practice known as patronage. The right to appoint a priest belonged to the person who controlled the living, usually a bishop or large

This aristocratic Oxford student is dressed for boating.

landowner. Only young men with connections in high places could hope to win the favor of such a patron. A squire or aristocrat with a living at his disposal might give it to a relative, a former schoolmate, or a friend of the family. If he needed money, he might even sell the living. The gentleman-priest who owed his living to a patron was far more likely to identify with the upper classes than with the poor families of the parish. One pamphlet aimed at farm laborers described the Anglican clergy as "prudent people" who were "to a certain extent slaves of their rich patrons, the lords and squires, and therefore have stood by them as they hardly dare stand up for you."

Despite all the flaws in church practices, there had always been dedicated clergymen who devoted their lives to their religious duties. As the Victorian Age progressed, reformers within the Anglican Church worked to instill the same sort of devotion throughout the clergy. Religious colleges were founded or expanded, providing priests with better education and training. At the same time, the church answered the need for more clergy by ordaining a number of gifted men who were not university graduates.

Many of the young priests who entered the ministry in Victorian times were inspired by the spiritual principles of the High Church revival, the social consciousness of the Broad Church movement, or the Gospel-centered mission of the Evangelicals. These energetic clergymen restored their churches and expanded their ministries. They reached out to the poor and working classes in troubled urban parishes. By the mid-1800s, Anglican churchmen were already reflecting on a "new spirit" in the ministry. The Reverend G. A. Selwyn, returning from an overseas post in 1854, remarked on the "great and visible change" that had taken place "in the thirteen years since I left England. It is now a very rare thing to see a careless clergyman [or] a neglected parish."

HODGE AND THE NEW VICAR

Not everyone applauded the new spirit that invigorated the Anglican Church in the nineteenth century. The people of quiet villages sometimes regarded the changes in age-old church practices with hostility, suspicion, or indifference. In the book *Hodge and His Masters*, the Victorian writer Richard Jefferies described the reaction of one rural community to an energetic new vicar. ("Hodge" was a widely used nickname for an agricultural laborer.)

The vicar's innovations were really most inoffensive. . . . The fault lay in the fact that they were innovations, so far as the practice of that parish was concerned. So the old folk raised their voices in a chorus of horror, and when they met gossiped over the awful downfall of the faith. All that the vicar had yet done was to intone [sing] a part of the service, and at once many announced that they should stay away.

Next he introduced a choir. The sweet voices of the white-robed boys rising along the vaulted roof of the old church melted the hearts of those who . . . ventured to go and hear them. . . . The church filled more and more every Sunday, and people came from the farthest corners of the parish, walking miles to listen. . . .

The [vicar's] . . . gentle, pleasing manner, with the sense of intellectual power behind it, quite overcame the old folk. They all [began to speak] with complacent pride of "our vicar"; and, what was more, opened their purses. The interior of the church was restored, and a noble organ built. . . . A large proportion of the upper and middle class of the parish was, without a doubt, now gathered around him. . . .

But what said Hodge to it all? Hodge said nothing. . . . The strong, sturdy men, the carters and shepherds, stood aloof; the bulk and backbone of the agricultural labouring population were not in the least affected. . . . They cleaned their boots on a Sunday morning while the bells were ringing, and walked down to their allotments [garden plots], and came home and ate their cabbage, and were as oblivious of the vicar as the wind that blew. They had no present quarrel with the Church; no complaint whatever; nor apparently any old memory or grudge; yet there was a something, a blank space as it were, between them and the Church.

Choirboys raise their voices in song, in a Victorian Christmas card.

COUNTRY PRIEST, CITY PRIEST

The Anglican priest was an important figure in the country community. Whether his income was large or small, he enjoyed a high social standing. His responsibilities included conducting worship services in the parish church and presiding over ceremonies such as baptisms, weddings, and funerals. He visited the poor and sick in their cottages. He supervised the village school. Cottagers turned to him for advice and assistance in matters such as understanding a legal document or writing an important letter. Like country squires, some rural parsons were also justices of the peace, although this practice gradually declined during the Victorian era. Clergy-justices were renowned—and sometimes despised—for their zeal in upholding the law and handing out stiff sentences to wrongdoers.

More popular was the priest's traditional role in a variety of social and charitable projects: organizing church get-togethers, setting up lending libraries and adult education classes, establishing clothing and coal clubs, which helped poor laborers put aside a little money each week for necessities. During the Victorian Age, the new spirit in the Anglican Church inspired the clergy to even greater activity. Some pastors worked to improve conditions in the overcrowded, unsanitary laborers' cottages. One vicar paid for the digging of new wells when a village's water supply became contaminated. Another broke up his parsonage farmlands into small allotments, which he rented out at low rates to landless cottagers.

Anglican clergymen also strived to relieve suffering and spread God's word in the cities. Urban pastors supervised Sunday schools and day schools. They pressed city leaders to build public parks, baths, and libraries. With the help of volunteers in parish organizations, they ran soup kitchens, orphanages, and visiting societies.

The Reverend John Cale Miller, a leading Evangelical rector in Birmingham, established a workingman's association that offered educational lectures, discussion groups, reading rooms, savings clubs, and tea-and-music parties. Miller's goal was "the cultivation and exercise of sympathy with the Working Classes." He recognized that the charity offered by the church was "too often insulting in its very patronage and condescension [air of superiority]. . . . We must go among them; we must improve their dwellings; we must provide them the means not only of mental self-improvement, but of physical recreation."

MINISTERS AND MISSIONS

Despite the best efforts of reform-minded Anglican clergymen, a gulf still separated them from the working classes. The priests of the established church were gentlemen, with close ties to the privileged classes. The minister of a Nonconformist church, on the other hand, usually came from a lower level of society. "Instead of dining with the squire, he goes out to tea with the tenant," observed the British journalist and editor Peter Anderson Graham. "People who would never think of presuming to ask the rector to eat with them will familiarly invite the Minister to take 'pot luck' at table."

While the practices of Nonconformist churches varied, in most cases individual congregations selected their own clergyman, known as the pastor or minister. Some ministers were educated in theological schools or seminaries. Others were self-educated. Members of the "laity" also played a prominent role in many Dissenting sects, such as the Methodists and Quakers. Lay ministers were not officially part of the clergy, but they were authorized to teach and lead worship services. In the 1880s Methodist lay preachers traveled across the countryside in horse-drawn caravans,

A minister baptizes abandoned infants in the chapel of a London orphanage.

conducting "revival" meetings—enthusiastic worship services featuring sermons, singing, and prayers, which were held in tents and rural chapels.

Relations between Nonconformist ministers and Anglican priests were often strained. While the priest was inclined to uphold the existing order, the minister was more likely to support government and social reforms. Ministers also called for an end to the traditional privileges of the established church. The conflicts between church and chapel occasionally erupted in nasty schemes against the members of rival congregations. In the county of Devon, an Anglican clergyman-justice teamed up with local farmers to deny jobs and relief payments to Methodists. Farther east in Buckinghamshire, Anglicans complained that Dissenting tradesmen made a point of "having the poor people in their debt and so compel them to attend the [Nonconformist] Meeting Houses."

There was at least one area in which Anglican and Nonconformist clergy agreed: it was their Christian duty to help the poor and suffering. In these efforts the priests had an edge over the ministers, thanks to the Anglican Church's greater wealth and organizational structure. In most cases, Nonconformist pastors were left to address local challenges on their own. Many pastors worked hard to raise funds to build new chapels and found charitable missions in the cities.

From time to time, churchmen and Dissenters cooperated in urban service projects. In London, for example, Evangelical Anglicans and Nonconformists joined together to form the London City Mission. Home Bible readings sponsored by this joint organization in 1860 reached an estimated 375,000 people, more than 10 percent of the capital's population.

A mother prepares her daughter for a religious milestone—the ceremony at which the girl will take part in her first Holy Communion.

FOUR

WIVES *and* CHILDREN

The distinguishing characteristics of the female
are tenderness and compassion. These qualities,
when combined with active and persevering diligence,
and stimulated by love to her Divine Saviour,
will render the services of the Clergyman's wife
highly useful to her husband.

HINTS TO A CLERGYMAN'S WIFE (1838)

THE VICTORIANS BELIEVED THAT MEN WERE THE
natural leaders of society, while women were more suited for the
"private sphere" of home and family. Despite these confining expec-
tations, many thousands of Victorian women played a major role in
church activities. Women were also their children's first teachers,
entrusted with the task of instilling "Christian virtues" such as faith
and obedience.

THE LADY OF THE PARSONAGE

Only men could serve as priests in the Church of England. An Anglican clergyman was expected to marry, and his wife—like the wife of any prominent Victorian—was responsible for running the household, entertaining guests, and raising the children. She was also an important part of her husband's ministry. As an advice book for clergymen's wives explained, a woman's "natural" qualities of sympathy and self-sacrifice made her ideal for the "private . . . walks of Christian love and benevolence [charity]." She could visit the sick, providing "*spiritual* as well as *temporal* [physical] benefit." She could teach the girls in the Sunday school (leaving the boys to her husband). She could hold classes for the young women of the parish, with the aim of "interesting their minds, awakening their consciences, and instructing their hearts." Inspired by "her love to her God and Saviour, and her desire to promote the spiritual and temporal welfare of her husband's parish," the dutiful wife would never waste her "precious hours in the gratification of personal vanity." Instead, "every moment of the day must have its appropriate employment; every hour must bring with it its own portion of allotted duty."

Victorian journals and letters show that the wives of many clergymen took this advice to heart. The lady of the parsonage typically assisted her husband in a wide variety of projects: arranging church socials and "penny readings"; overseeing the local school; acting as treasurer for the savings clubs and coal clubs set up for poor laborers; visiting the poor, sick, and elderly. In a small parish, she usually visited all the families herself. In large urban districts, she might organize the upper- and middle-class women into visiting societies. The volunteers visited an assigned group of dwellings, inquiring into the people's welfare. They might bring gifts of food, blankets, or clothing. They might read aloud from the Bible or a religious pamphlet. In

The lady of the parsonage oversees poor parishioners at a Bible reading.

cases of severe hardship, the visiting ladies could arrange for a parishioner to be admitted to a hospital, almshouse (a privately funded home for the poor), or some other charitable institution.

WOMEN'S FAITH IN ACTION

While men headed up nearly all the Victorian religious charities, it was middle-class women who did most of the day-to-day work. Women were especially active in fund-raising. They organized countless charity teas, concerts, and fairs, or bazaars. They contributed an endless flood of handicrafts for sale at the bazaars: dried flower arrangements, stitched samplers, painted picture frames, beaded pen wipers, embroidered handkerchiefs, slippers, and suspenders. They staffed the booths and persuaded shoppers to buy all the pretty knickknacks. Charitable activities such as these offered "respectable" women a rare chance to display their artistic talents and gain skills in areas such as administration, sales, and accounting. A few women put their new experience to work in organizing their own female-run charitable institutions, including societies for the care of widows and orphans.

Women also supported mission work. The Church of England and a number of Nonconformist sects sent missionaries to spread Christianity in India, Africa, China, and other "less civilized" parts of the world. Women were active in the mission societies that raised funds to support the foreign missions. Some became missionaries themselves, either on their own or in company with their husbands. Female missionaries were often better than men at understanding the needs of the women of other cultures. During the late 1800s, female missionaries in India led a drive to establish clinics and hospitals where Indian women (whose culture barred them from visiting male doctors) could receive medical care from Western-trained "lady doctors."

Some women devoted their faith and talents to the Salvation Army. Organized by Catherine and William Booth in 1878, this Evangelical Christian organization ministered to the poor in London and other cities. The Salvation Army held open-air religious services, established shelters and soup kitchens, and campaigned for better wages and working conditions for women and children. The female and male "officers" in charge of these activities had equal rights and responsibilities.

Victorian women also served as ministers in a number of Nonconformist churches. By the end of Queen Victoria's reign, there were nearly five thousand female ministers in England and Wales. One of the most notable early nineteenth-century women preachers was Elizabeth Gurney Fry. This reformist Quaker founded a mission that set up chapels in women's prisons, helped female inmates earn income by making goods for sale, and ran schools for children who lived with their mothers in prison. Queen Victoria was a great admirer of Elizabeth Fry's work, inviting her to court and donating money to her cause.

While the Church of England did not ordain female priests, the late 1800s saw the first women enter its ranks as deaconesses. The church also allowed women to found religious communities known as sisterhoods. Like the nuns in Roman Catholic convents, Anglican sisters devoted their lives to serving God by helping the poor. They founded schools, orphanages, hospitals, women's shelters, and other community services, mainly in London but also in other cities and rural areas. Unlike Catholic convents, the Anglican sisterhoods were mostly self-supporting, carrying out their work with little or no help from the church. By the end of the nineteenth century, some ten thousand women had lived in one of the eighty or so sisterhoods, making these independent communities the largest all-female institutions in Victorian England.

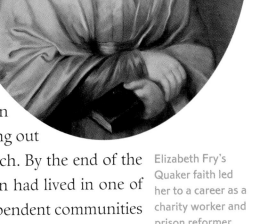

Elizabeth Fry's Quaker faith led her to a career as a charity worker and prison reformer.

RAISED IN THE CHURCH

Regardless of their family's faith, most Victorian children grew up in the arms of the Church of England. Before 1870 the Anglican Church operated about nine-tenths of England's elementary schools. (The rest were connected with the Catholic Church or one of the Nonconformist sects, mainly the Wesleyan Methodists or Congregationalists.) The Elementary Education Act of 1870 required the government to provide funds for establishing "board schools" in areas where there were no religious or charitable schools. Still, by the end of the nineteenth century, more than 60 percent of all elementary schools in England and Wales were connected with the Church of England.

Religious instruction was a regular part of a Victorian schoolchild's education. Scripture lessons were usually provided by the local Anglican priest or his curate. In Flora Thompson's village, the rector came to school at ten o'clock each morning to read from the Bible and listen to the children

reciting from memory the names of the kings of Israel and repeating the Church Catechism [questions and answers on church doctrine]. After that, he would deliver a little lecture on morals and behaviour. The children must not lie or steal or be discontented or envious. God had placed them just where they were in the social order and given them their own special work to do; to envy others or to try to change their own lot in life was a sin of which he hoped they would never be guilty.

As part of their Christian education, many Victorian children were taught to say grace before meals.

These moral lectures reinforced the lessons that many children, particularly those of the middle class, got at home. Mothers taught their children religion and morality along with reading, writing, and other academic subjects. Molly Hughes, who grew up in Victorian London, recalled that her mother began each day's schooling by opening "an enormous Bible. It was invariably at the Old Testament, and I had to read aloud." Molly's science lessons came from a text with information such as: "Q. What should a fearful person do to be secure in a storm? A. Draw his bedstead into the middle of the room, commit himself to the care of God, and go to bed."

For many children religious instruction continued into the weekend. Anglican day schools commonly required students to attend Sunday services at the parish church, as well as Sunday school. One girl from a village in eastern England recalled a monotonous routine of "Matins [morning prayers] in the morning, Sunday school in the afternoon, and Evensong [evening services] at night." But Sunday school was not always dreary. In areas without a regular school, it might offer the only opportunity for children to get a basic education in reading and writing. An annual outing to the seaside also gave poor and working-class youngsters a chance to have fun and see the wider world.

Surprisingly, despite all the emphasis on religious instruction, a good number of Victorian children had little or no knowledge of the Christian faith. In the cities especially, poor and working-class children might grow up without ever entering a church or chapel. Somewhere along the way, they usually picked up a mishmash of religious names and concepts. A government investigator who interviewed young factory workers in Birmingham reported that, for many of the children,

the state of mind as regards the simplest facts of religion is dark almost beyond belief. It is not too much to say that to many, God, the Bible, the Saviour, a Christian, even a future [after-death] state, are ideas entirely or all but unknown. God is "a good man," or "the man in heaven"; "I've heerd [of Christ], but don't know *what it is*". . . . Heaven was heard of only "when father died long ago, mother said he was going there." Some think that bad and good go there alike, or on the other hand, that "them as is wicked shall be worshiped, that means shall all go to hell."

JESSICA'S FIRST PRAYER

The Victorian Age saw a flowering of children's literature. Among the many books written especially for children were adventure tales (such as Robert Louis Stevenson's *Treasure Island*), school stories (Thomas Hughes's *Tom Brown's Schooldays*), and nonsense writing (Lewis Carroll's *Alice's Adventures in Wonderland*). There were also a host of books and periodicals that aimed to instill religious faith and morality in young readers. One of the most popular religious novels for children was *Jessica's First Prayer*, written by Hesba Stretton (the pen name of Sarah Smith) in 1867. This sentimental novel tells the story of a poor city girl whose innocent trust in God leads a greedy man to salvation. In the following passage, the man (Daniel) visits Jessica as she lies gravely ill in a miserable slum tenement.

Above: A deathbed scene, from an 1860 magazine illustration

"Oh!" she cried, gladly, but in a feeble voice, "it's Mr. Dan'el! Has God told you to come here, Mr. Dan'el?"

"Yes," said Daniel, kneeling beside her, taking her wasted hand in his, and parting the matted hair upon her damp forehead.

"What did he say to you, Mr. Dan'el?" said Jessica.

"He told me I was a great sinner," replied Daniel. "He told me I loved a little bit of dirty money better than a poor, friendless, helpless child, whom he had sent to me to see if I would do her a little good for his sake. . . ."

"Why don't you ask him to make you good for Jesus Christ's sake?" asked the child.

"I can't," he said. "I've been kneeling down Sunday after Sunday when the minister's been praying, but all the time I was thinking how rich some of the carriage people were. I've been loving money and worshipping money all along, and I've nearly let you die rather than run the risk of losing part of my earnings. I'm a very sinful man."

"But you know what the minister often says," murmured Jessica. "'Herein is love, not that we loved God, but that he loved us, and sent his Son to be the propitiation for our sins.'"

"I've heard it so often that I don't feel it," said Daniel. "I used to like to hear the minister say it, but now it goes in at one ear and out at the other. My heart is very hard, Jessica."

By the feeble glimmer of the candle Daniel saw Jessica's wistful eyes fixed upon him with a sad and loving glance; and then she lifted up her weak hand to her face, and laid it over her closed eyelids, and her feverish lips moved slowly.

"God," she said, "please to make Mr. Dan'el's heart soft, for Jesus Christ's sake, Amen."

A housemaid carries a flaming plum pudding, highlight of the Victorian Christmas dinner.

FIVE

CELEBRATING THE FAITH

Every Sunday, morning and afternoon,
the two cracked, flat-toned bells at the church
in the mother village called the faithful to worship.
Ding-dong, Ding-dong, Ding-dong, they went,
and, when they heard them, the hamlet churchgoers
hurried across fields and over stiles.

∽ FLORA THOMPSON, *LARK RISE TO CANDLEFORD*

CHRISTIAN RITUALS AND CELEBRATIONS TOUCHED THE life of nearly every Victorian. Sunday was the Lord's Day, observed in accordance with social conventions and religious and government laws. Religious festivals were a time for fun, family, and feasting. The most popular festival of all was Christmas. The Victorians transformed this simple church holiday into a national celebration. In fact, in many ways Christmas as we celebrate it today was a Victorian invention.

REMEMBERING THE SABBATH

"Sunday in London in the rain," wrote the French historian Hippolyte Taine, on a visit to the capital in the mid-1800s. "The shops are shut, the streets almost deserted; the aspect is that of an immense and a well-ordered cemetery."

The sometimes-gloomy aspect of a Victorian Sunday was the result of an Evangelical movement known as Sabbatarianism. Sabbatarians placed great emphasis on the biblical commandment to "remember the Sabbath day, and keep it holy." In their view Sundays should be devoted entirely to religion. All work was forbidden. So were all forms of pleasure and recreation. During the early 1850s, members of an Evangelical organization called the Lord's Day Observance Society pressed for the strict enforcement of old laws and the passage of new ones limiting public pastimes on the Christian Sabbath. Their campaign succeeded in closing public parks, theaters, museums, art galleries, zoos, and most retail businesses (with the notable exception of pubs) on Sunday.

Many non-Evangelical families, including those that were not particularly religious, picked up the practice of Sabbatarianism. No respectable middle-class Victorian would dream of playing cards, drawing, embroidering, playing music (except for hymns), or reading a novel on Sunday. Parents put away their children's playthings, with the possible exception of religious-themed toys such as a wooden Noah's ark. For some families these Sunday observances were a sincere reflection of religious convictions. For others they were more about appearances. Gwen Raverat, who came from a large upper-class family in Cambridge, England, remembered that "there were many things we might not do, not because they were wrong in themselves, but 'because of the maids.' We might never sew or knit or play cards at all . . . ; and when we went out to play tennis, we used to

THE CHURCH

48

make our rackets into brown-paper parcels, to avoid giving offence to the people in the street!"

A family gives thanks before sitting down to a light Sunday supper.

Over time the power of the Sabbatarian movement declined. Critics objected to the laws that prevented working men and women from enjoying innocent activities such as strolling in the park on their one day of leisure. They also condemned the double standard that restricted poor and working-class pleasures, while the wealthy were free to ride their carriages and hold dinner parties on the Sabbath. By the end of the nineteenth century, museums and art galleries had begun to open their doors on Sunday afternoons, and the other barriers to public amusements were gradually falling.

PSALMS AND SERMONS

The most important Sunday observance, of course, was churchgoing. Anglican families often went to church twice, once in the morning and again in the mid-afternoon or early evening. The Bible readings, prayers, psalms, and sermons offered comfort and inspiration to countless men and women. Lucy Edwards of Eydon, a village in central England, was one of the many who "sang in the choir all the days of her life [and] loved the church with all her heart, mind and soul."

At the same time, as Flora Thompson recalled, Sunday services could seem "everlasting" to the children who "sat in their stiff, stuffy, best clothes, their stomachs lined with heavy Sunday dinner, in a kind of waking doze, through which . . . the Rector's voice buzzed beelike." Common themes for Anglican sermons included the evils of drinking, quarreling, and envy, and the virtues of working hard and never missing a church service. In Flora's church the rector "would hammer away" at the "duty of regular churchgoing . . . for forty-five minutes, never seeming to realize that he was preaching to the absent [who] were snoring upon their beds a mile and a half away."

Worship services in Nonconformist chapels were often more intensely personal than the Anglican services. When Flora attended Sunday evening services in the cottage of a Methodist neighbor, she enjoyed the simple but heartfelt sermons offered by the traveling preacher, often a farm laborer, crafts-

Flanked by the high walls of her wealthy family's private pew, a little girl dozes off during a long church sermon.

A SON'S SOMBER SUNDAY

Edmund Gosse, whose father was a lay preacher with a small, strict Nonconformist sect called the Plymouth Brethren, wrote about the wearisome Sundays of his childhood. Modern-day scholars suspect that Edmund's account may not be entirely accurate. However, his book does give us a compelling picture of life in a strict Sabbatarian household.

We came down to breakfast at the usual time. My Father prayed briefly before we began the meal; after it, the bell was rung, and, before the breakfast was cleared away, we had a lengthy service of exposition [a religious lecture] and prayer with the servants. If the weather was fine, we then walked about the garden doing nothing, for about half an hour. We then sat, each in a separate room, with our Bibles open and some commentary on the text beside us, and prepared our minds for the morning service. A little before 11 a.m. we sallied forth, carrying our Bibles and hymn-books, and went through the morning service of two hours at the [meeting] Room; this was the central event of Sunday.

We then came back to dinner; . . . and after it my Father and my stepmother took a nap, each in a different room. . . . In the middle of the afternoon, my stepmother and I proceeded up the village to Sunday school, where I was early promoted to the tuition of a few very little boys. We returned in time for tea, immediately after which we all marched forth, again armed as in the morning, with Bibles and hymn-books, and we went through the evening-service, at which my Father preached. The hour was now already past my week-day bedtime, but we had another service to attend, the Believers' Prayer Meeting, which commonly occupied forty minutes more. Then we used to creep home, I often so tired that the weariness was like a physical pain, and I was permitted, without further "worship", to slip upstairs to bed.

Above: A family enters their village church for Sunday services.

man, or small shopkeeper. Even more interesting were the testimonies of worshipers who stood up to confess their "mild sins." Sometimes members of the congregation broke out in long, rambling prayers that were really "one-sided conversations with the Deity"—such as "old Mr Barker telling God that it had not rained for a fortnight and that his carrot bed was getting 'mortal dry'; or that swine fever had broken out on a farm four miles away and that his own pig didn't seem 'no great shakes.'" Along with these lively diversions, the cottage services offered young Flora a welcome break from a dull Sunday evening at home, "with the whole family huddled round the fire . . . and no one allowed to speak and barely to move."

EASTER EGGS AND CHRISTMAS CAROLS

An annual round of church festivals offered the hardworking Victorians a chance to make merry while celebrating their faith. On Shrove Tuesday, observed in February or March, parishioners went to church to be "shriven," or forgiven for their sins, then enjoyed a hearty pancake supper. The day after Shrove Tuesday was the beginning of Lent. During this forty-day period of fasting and reflection, religious-minded people gave up rich food and other luxuries. Lent came to an end on Easter Sunday. This important Christian festival, celebrating Christ's resurrection from the dead, was marked with a special church service. Easter treats included special cakes, cookies, and chocolate eggs for the children.

Whitsunday (the seventh Sunday after Easter) commemorated the coming of the Holy Spirit to Christ's followers. Many country communities celebrated this springtime festival with games, processions, and a feast, sometimes paid for by the local squire. Summer was the time for the church "wake"—a festival honoring the founder or patron saint of the parish church.

Fall brought the harvest, traditionally celebrated with drinking, dancing, and other sometimes rowdy festivities. In Victorian times the church stepped in to offer a more well-mannered alternative: the harvest festival. Country harvest festivals combined a church service and supper with entertainments such as street fairs, ball games, merry-go-rounds, and family-friendly dances (where the only drinks served were nonalcoholic). An urban parish might celebrate harvesttime with a special service in a church decorated with fresh-picked fruits, vegetables, and flowers.

Winter brought the holiday of all holidays, Christmas. Before the Victorian Age, most Christians had celebrated the birth of Jesus simply, attending church and perhaps enjoying a special family dinner. The Victorians revived many older traditions: decorating with the ancient symbols of holly, ivy, and mistletoe; warming their hearths with a blazing Yule log; singing Christmas hymns in roving companies of "waits," or carolers. They also adopted new traditions, such as exchanging Christmas cards and decorating Christmas trees (a German custom imported by Prince Albert). Charles Dickens helped promote the Christmas spirit of goodwill and merriment in his magazine articles, short stories, and novels such as the ever-popular *A Christmas Carol*.

On Christmas Eve children's stockings were filled with nuts, chocolates, oranges, and, for the fortunate, a small gift or two. On Christmas Day many people, even those who were not regular churchgoers, attended a special worship service. After church, families sat down to a feast of roast goose, turkey, or beef, along with potatoes, applesauce, and other side dishes. Dessert was a plum pudding, doused with brandy and brought flaming to the table. Hidden inside the pudding were charms: a coin (foretelling riches), a ring (for marriage), a thimble or button (meaning the finder would remain

The Victorians decorated their Christmas trees with candles, small handmade gifts, glass globes, and other colorful ornaments.

single). Many poor and working-class families saved up all year for their special Christmas dinner. Others looked forward to the heaping Christmas basket donated by the local squire or farmer.

The day after Christmas was Boxing Day. Prosperous Victorians showed their Christmas spirit on this holiday by distributing boxes of food and used clothes to the poor. Many also gave money or gifts to their servants and tradesmen. William Tayler, a footman in the home of a wealthy London widow, described a merry, somewhat "fuddled" Boxing Day in 1837:

> We have had numbers here today—sweeps, beadles [minor parish officials], lamplighters, watermen, dustmen, scavengers—that is the men who clean the mud out of the streets—newspaper boy, general postmen, twopenny postmen

[who made special deliveries] and waits. These are a set of men that goe about the streets playing musick in the night after people are in bed and a sleepe. Some people are very fond of hearing them, but for my own part, I don't admire being roused from a sound sleep by a whole band of musick. . . . All these people expect to have a shilling or half a crown each. . . . I mite get fuddled [drunk] two or three times a day if I had a mind, as all the trades people that serve this house are very pressing with [a] glass of something to drink their health this Christmas time.

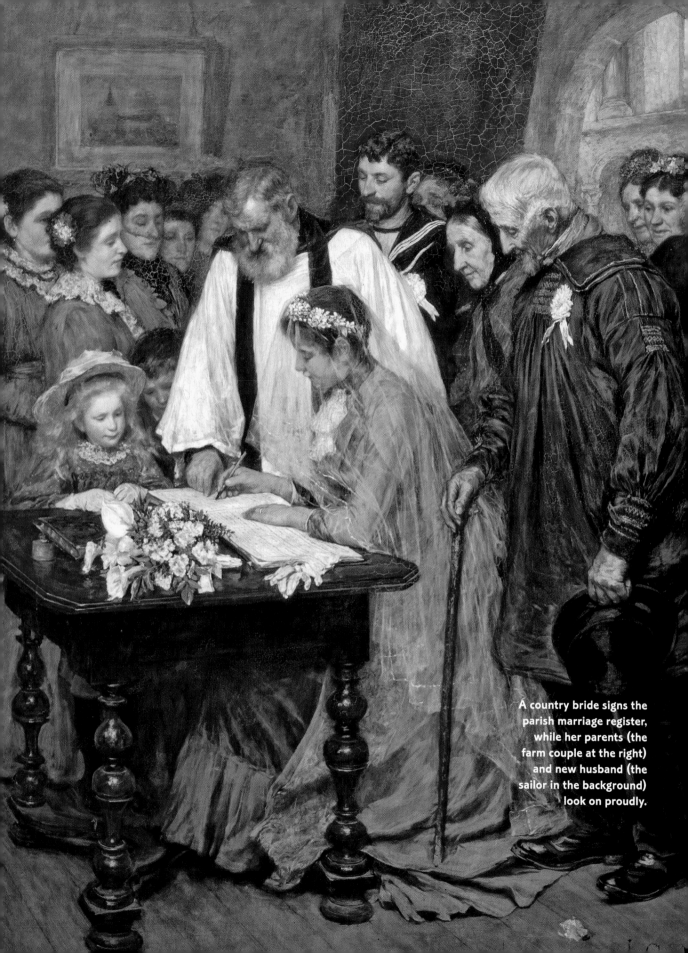

A country bride signs the parish marriage register, while her parents (the farm couple at the right) and new husband (the sailor in the background) look on proudly.

SIX

FROM CRADLE TO GRAVE

The sun was shining, the bells were chiming,
the church was filling. Happy was the bride that the
sun shone on. But all brides were happy!
∾ FRANCES HODGSON BURNETT,
THE ONE I KNEW THE BEST OF ALL (1893)

RELIGIOUS AND NONRELIGIOUS VICTORIANS ALIKE
went to church to observe the major milestones of life. Baptisms and
weddings were joyous occasions, celebrated simply or in grand style,
depending on the family's wealth and social standing. Funerals were
often elaborate, expensive affairs. Following the funeral came a
mourning period with rules so complex that some Victorians con-
sulted books and magazines to make sure they wore the right clothes
for each stage of their grief.

NEWBORNS AND NEWLYWEDS

Most Victorian parents, even those who were not particularly religious, took their newborns to church to be baptized. In this ancient ritual, the pastor dipped the infant in water, ritually cleansing it of sin and making it part of the Christian church. Friends or relatives served as godparents, promising to help raise the child in the Christian faith. Adults could also be baptized. Some Nonconformist churches, such as the Baptists, believed that only adult baptism was valid, because only adults were old enough to claim the faith for themselves.

At age fourteen or fifteen, a child could be confirmed (although this practice was less common than baptism). Through confirmation the child ratified or "confirmed" the commitment to Christ that had been made on his or her behalf at baptism. In the Anglican Church, the bishop of the diocese laid his hands on the confirmation candidate, formally receiving the boy or girl as an adult member of the church.

Victorian girls affirm their Christian faith through the rite of confirmation.

The next major event in most young people's lives was marriage. Regardless of their faith, the great majority of Victorian couples married in the Church of England. The couple visited the parish clergyman and asked him to "publish the banns," or inform the public of their intention to marry, by announcing it from the church pulpit. If after three Sunday announcements no one had spoken out against the proposed union, the couple was free to marry.

Until 1880 English law required all church weddings to take place before noon (later extended to 3 p.m.) Many lower and middle-class Victorians simply went to their parish church, where the priest joined them in marriage, with their parents and a few close friends as witnesses. After the ceremony the new couple celebrated with a special wedding breakfast.

Upper-class weddings were far more fancy. A well-to-do couple could avoid having their names read out in church (often considered "common") by purchasing a marriage license. Men and women of the nobility had the added privilege of asking the archbishop for a "special license." This costly document not only let the couple avoid the banns but gave them the option of marrying in a fashionable church outside their home parish.

The fashionable bride wore an expensive gown (white was traditional by the end of the century), a white veil, and a wreath of orange blossoms. She was attended by up to twelve bridesmaids in similar, but not necessarily identical, gowns. The groom and his attendant, usually a brother or close friend, wore coats of dark blue, wine-red, purple, or black, with pale-colored trousers. One or two little boys might act as pages, holding up the trailing skirt of the bridal gown.

After the ceremony the couple and their guests enjoyed a wedding "breakfast" (really a multicourse dinner). Then the bride changed into her traveling clothes, and the couple departed for their wedding trip. In the later part of the Victorian period, slippers were tied to the back of the carriage, and the guests threw rice, a symbol of fertility.

Some Anglican clergymen disapproved of the increasingly expensive trappings of upper-class weddings. In 1854 the Reverend Benjamin Armstrong of Norfolk wrote in his diary:

> The mind reverts to the new well-fitting gloves and bouquets imported from Covent Garden [in London]. . . . A handsome breakfast with lots of champagne—wretched speeches on the part of the men and tears on the part of the women. Then come the corded [gift] boxes; the bridegroom has another glass; an old shoe is thrown into the carriage for luck and off they go. For my own part I dislike weddings and would [rather] attend a funeral.

A GOOD DEATH

Father Armstrong must have had many opportunities to indulge his preference for funerals. Life was fragile in Victorian times, amid the widespread perils of poor nutrition, poor sanitation, epidemic diseases, and inadequate or ineffective medical care. In 1850 the life expectancy of a person born in England or Wales was only about forty years, and more than one child in ten died before his or her first birthday.

Most Victorians died at home. In the ideal "Christian death," a man or woman died surrounded by loved ones, after wrapping up all personal affairs and making peace with God. Victorian novelists put great stock in sentimental deathbed scenes, in which a character's dying words took on special significance. The importance attached to "famous last words" was not solely confined to fiction. In the 1850s Thomas Charles Geldart, a well-respected professor who had always been fond of a drink, died in his wife's arms, after exclaiming, "You will let the undergraduates have some of the old sherry." Horrified by her husband's less-than-spiritual farewell, the professor's widow had his body cut open and examined. She was relieved when the doctors told her to ignore his last words, because his mind had been clouded at death.

These well-bred young ladies wearing mourning dresses probably have lost a close relative, perhaps a mother or father.

After death a person's body usually remained at home until the funeral. In early Victorian times, funerals were flamboyant affairs, particularly among the upper and upper-middle classes. The coffin was draped in black velvet and carried on a carriage pulled by black horses with plumes of black feathers on their heads. Professional mourners known as "feathermen" walked before the hearse, each carrying a tray of waving black plumes. The undertaker also provided "mutes"—gloomy-faced mourners who wore giant black sashes and carried tall staffs tied with black ribbons. Male friends and family members wore top hats tied with black streamers called "weepers," while the ladies wore black mourning dresses. In country funerals men carried the coffin from the hearse into the church, where the pastor performed the funeral service. In large towns and cities, services were often held in a chapel at the cemetery.

Poor and working-class Victorians struggled to afford the costs of a decent funeral. It was a great disgrace to resort to a "pauper's funeral," paid for by the parish. Many working people contributed a penny a week to a burial club, which would pay for their coffin and

Two men carry a small coffin during a simple country funeral.

other expenses when they died. Country laborers often cut down on expenses by burying their loved ones with "walking funerals." In place of the horse-drawn hearse, the men of the village carried the coffin on their shoulders—sometimes as far as two miles from the home to the church to the graveyard.

During the 1850s, reform groups including the National Funeral and Mourning Association worked to encourage greater moderation in burial practices. Through their efforts undertakers were forced to offer simpler, less costly alternatives to the lavish Victorian funeral. Many people welcomed the change. Others feared that a less-than-impressive funeral would make their family seem disrespectful or cheap. In 1876 Jeannette Marshall, a young upper-middle-class Londoner, was appalled by the "simple" arrangements that her father and uncles made in burying her grandmother. "The funeral was *without* mourning coaches, scarves or hatbands," she complained.

Every one going in their own carriage. In order that people shd. [should] not think it was meanness [cheapness] that prompted them to do so, they had four horses to the hearse, and a very handsome polished oak coffin. It is so horrible, the idea of saving every penny of what one's relations have left.

AFTER THE FUNERAL

Victorian mourning rituals could be as complicated as the most elaborate funeral. Even poor women were expected to wear "widow's weeds" (often a regular dress dyed black) as a sign of grief for their departed husbands. Among the middle and upper classes, detailed rules (more strict for women than for men) governed which clothes were appropriate for the different stages of mourning, how long each stage should last, and how soon the mourner could reenter society. A Victorian etiquette book called *Manners and Rules of Good Society* offered guidelines for mourning various family members, from husbands and parents to great-aunts and second cousins. As this extract from a later edition of the book (published in 1913) suggests, the rules of mourning gradually relaxed in the late nineteenth and early twentieth centuries.

The Various Periods of Mourning for relatives have within the last few years been materially shortened, and the change generally accepted; but as some still prefer to adhere to the longest periods prescribed by custom, in the present chapter both periods are given. . . .

Longest Period for a Widow's Mourning is two years. The shorter period is eighteen months. Formerly crape [a dull silk fabric] was worn for one year and nine months; for the first twelve months the dress was entirely covered with crape. The newer fashion in widows' mourning is to wear crape as a trimming only, and to discontinue its wear after six or eight months. . . .

After the first year white neckbands and white strings to the bonnet may be worn. Also hats in place of bonnets. Further touches of white may follow during the next three months. . . .

For a Parent the period of mourning is twelve months. . . . The black may be relieved with touches of white after three months. Crape is optional; many prefer not to wear it at all, others as a trimming. . . .

For a Brother or Sister, the longest period of mourning is six months, the shortest period four months. . .

Much Latitude [flexibility] is allowed to Men with regard to the foregoing periods of mourning. A [black] Hat-band should be worn during the whole of each period, but it is not imperative to wear suits of black longer than half the periods given, save [except] in the case of widowers.

Above: This memorial brooch would have helped surviving family members remember a lost loved one.

Charles Darwin turned the Victorian world upside down with his theory of evolution.

SEVEN

A CRISIS
of FAITH

There is not a creed which is not shaken,
not an accredited dogma [system of beliefs] which is not
shown to be questionable, not a received tradition which does not
threaten to dissolve. Our religion has materialised itself
in the fact, in the supposed fact; it has attached its emotion
to the fact, and now the fact is failing it.
— MATTHEW ARNOLD, "THE STUDY OF POETRY" (1880)

LIKE COUNTLESS GENERATIONS BEFORE THEM, THE
Victorians found consolation and meaning in their religious faith.
But the powerful forces that swept the Victorian Age did not leave
religion untouched. We have seen how the churches scrambled to
keep pace with England's fast-growing, fast-changing society. At the
same time, advances in science and scholarship were shaking the very
foundations of Christian belief.

THE "HAMMERS" OF SCIENCE

Science as we know it today came of age during the Victorian period. At the start of the nineteenth century, a person who was interested in what we call science would study "natural philosophy," a broad field that included all of nature and the physical universe. Natural philosophers used reason and logical arguments to explain the mysteries of the physical world. England was home to a small number of full-time natural philosophers, along with many "amateur scientists"—mostly middle-class men and women who enjoyed hobbies such as collecting and classifying fossils, shells, plants, and other specimens.

In the early 1800s, natural philosophers began to replace guesswork with what became known as the scientific method. Developed centuries earlier—most likely by Muslim scholars in North Africa, the Middle East, and Spain—the scientific method relies on careful observations and experiments to prove or disprove theories about the natural world. Western scientists using this "new" method were responsible for many of the scientific and technological advances of the Victorian Age. The English public eagerly followed the latest discoveries in geology, chemistry, bacteriology, and other scientific disciplines. By the late nineteenth century, science had developed into a widely respected field of knowledge, studied by increasing numbers of students at public schools, universities, and technical schools.

No one could deny the benefits of a discovery that led to the development of X-rays or electric lightbulbs. Some scientific advances were more controversial, however. Geologists who studied rock layers and fossils announced that the earth was many millions of years old. That was a shock to the majority of Victorians who accepted traditional interpretations of the Bible, which put the planet's age at about six thousand years. Discoveries of prehistoric

stone tools and human remains led scientists to conclude that early human beings had lived alongside now-extinct animals at different stages of the earth's long history. Those findings contradicted the biblical stories of the creation and early history of humankind. Also troubling was the fact that geologists could find no evidence of the Great Flood described in the book of Genesis, which was said to have covered the earth in the days of Noah.

Nineteenth-century German scholars added further fuel to the Victorians' religious doubts. When these scholars compared events described in the Bible to historical records and geological discoveries, they found numerous contradictions. Many became convinced that the Bible was not the infallible word of God but simply a collection of ancient histories, biographies, prayers, songs, and myths. Scholars who specialized in language also pointed to errors in the way the official King James Version of the Bible translated the ancient Hebrew texts. Their investigations led to a new translation, the English Revised Version.

Michael Faraday, inventor of the electric motor, at work in his laboratory. Discoveries made by Faraday and other nineteenth-century scientists transformed English society.

All these challenges to the time-honored teachings of the Bible left the Victorians divided and shaken. Many looked back in longing to a time before historians and scientists called their most fundamental beliefs into question. "If only the Geologists would let me alone, I could do very well," wrote the artist and philosopher John Ruskin in 1851, "but those dreadful Hammers! I hear the clink of them at the end of every cadence of the Bible verses." Sentiments such as these set the stage for the greatest religious controversy of the nineteenth century: the bombshell that was Charles Darwin's theory of evolution.

ON THE ORIGIN OF SPECIES

In 1831 a young Englishman named Charles Darwin set sail on the survey ship HMS *Beagle*. Darwin had spent his college years studying religion, medicine, and geology, but his real passion was natural history—a field of science concerned with the development of living things. During the *Beagle*'s five-year expedition to South America and the islands of the South Seas, Darwin observed and collected specimens of plants, insects, and animals, as well as fossils from long-extinct creatures. After returning to England, he spent more than twenty years studying his collections, testing his findings, and writing up his ideas. In 1859 he finally published *On the Origin of Species by Means of Natural Selection*. It was an instant best seller. It was also one of the most controversial books ever written.

On the Origin of Species explained the process of evolution. Darwin was not the first scientist to introduce this concept, but he *was* the first to offer a convincing explanation of how evolution occurred and to base his explanation on a mountain of scientific evidence. New species evolve, he wrote, through a process called natural selection. All parents pass along their characteristics to their offspring, along

Charles Darwin spent nearly five years sailing around the globe on the survey ship HMS *Beagle*.

with slight changes, or variations. The offspring with variations that help them survive in their natural environment are the ones that live long enough to reproduce. For example, a bird born with an extra-long beak would be better than its shorter-beaked relatives at plucking insects from deep cracks in trees and rocks. That would make it more likely to survive and become a parent itself, passing on its long beak to the next generation. Over time a species accumulates many different variations. Eventually a bird would evolve with features that made it so different from its original ancestor that it would be considered a new species.

While *On the Origin of Species* carefully avoided the topic of human origins, readers had no trouble making the connection between evolution and humankind. Many were outraged. The idea that people were nothing more than highly developed animals called the central beliefs of Christianity into question. Bishop Samuel Wilberforce

A CRISIS OF FAITH

DARWIN'S GRAND VIEW

Charles Darwin knew that his theory of evolution would send shock waves through Victorian society. While he believed that humans were subject to the same laws of natural selection as other animals, he did not make that argument in *On the Origin of Species*. The following passage from that book's conclusion includes its only sentence touching on "the origin of man," couched in terms that were meant to reassure fellow Christians. Twelve years later, Darwin would tackle the topic of human evolution head-on in another groundbreaking volume, *The Descent of Man*.

In the future I see open fields for far more important researches. . . . Light will be thrown on the origin of man and his history. . . .

It is interesting to contemplate a tangled bank, clothed with many plants of many kinds, with birds singing on the bushes, with various insects flitting about, and with worms crawling through the damp earth, and to reflect that these elaborately constructed forms, so different from each other, and dependent on each other in so complex a manner, have all been produced by laws acting around us. . . . Thus, from the war of nature, from famine and death, the most exalted object which we are capable of conceiving, namely, the production of the higher animals, directly follows. There is grandeur in this view of life, with its several powers, having been originally breathed by the Creator into a few forms or into one; and that, whilst this planet has gone cycling on according to the fixed law of gravity, from so simple a beginning endless forms most beautiful and most wonderful have been, and are being evolved.

Above: Darwin used the orchid—a complicated flower with thousands of different varieties—to illustrate his theory of evolution.

denounced Darwin's "speculations" as "absolutely incompatible" with the Bible's teachings regarding the

> moral and spiritual condition of man. . . . Man's derived [God-given] supremacy over the earth; man's power of articulate speech; man's gift of reason; man's free will and responsibility; man's fall and man's redemption; the incarnation of the Eternal Son [the union of God and man in the body of Christ]; the indwelling of the Eternal Spirit—all are equally and utterly irreconcilable with the degrading notion of the brute origin of him who was created in the image of God, and redeemed by the Eternal Son.

SIGNS OF THE TIMES

In 1860 the noted English scientist Thomas Henry Huxley spoke out in defense of Charles Darwin's theory of evolution. "The Origin of Species," Huxley wrote, "is not the first, and it will not be the last of the great questions born of science, which will demand settlement from this generation. The general mind is seething strangely, and to those who watch the signs of the times, it seems plain that this nineteenth century will see revolutions of thought and practice."

As the Victorian Age drew to a close, Huxley's words seemed prophetic indeed. The religious community had faced many challenges in the course of the century, calling forth new practices and new ways of thought. Anglican leaders had seen their influence decline as the power of Dissent rose. Evangelicals had injected new life into both Anglican and Dissenting churches with their zeal for good works. At the same time, clergy in all branches of Christianity had struggled to counter a rising wave of religious indifference. Despite their determined efforts to reach the masses in England's teeming cities, that battle was far from won. A survey in 1902 found that only one out of every five Londoners attended church on Sunday, a sharp decline from the already troubling figures of the 1851 religious census.

No challenge was greater than the questions raised by the work of the scientists and biblical scholars. Christians reacted in different ways to the many assaults on their religious beliefs. Some held fast to their faith in the literal truth of the Bible. Others suffered doubt and despair. After long soul-searching, a number of Victorians turned their backs on religion and searched for meaning in other areas of life: work, family, philosophy, social service based on "Christian ethics" stripped of Christian beliefs.

There were also many Victorians who found a way to reconcile their old beliefs with new ideas. The Bible's six days of creation became six long periods of time. Evolution was hailed as just one more illustration of God's marvelous handiwork. Scientists such as Thomas Huxley argued that "reverence is the handmaid of knowledge"—that a Christian could honor God through a thorough scientific study of His works. Many others maintained that true Christianity did not depend on the Bible's historical accuracy but on its eternal spiritual truths.

Meanwhile, millions of Queen Victoria's subjects paid no attention at all to the arguments of scientists, scholars, and churchmen. These ordinary men and women read their Bibles and said their prayers. They baptized their babies and went to church on Easter, Christmas, and (more or less often) on Sunday. They took comfort in the religion of their parents and grandparents, and they passed it down to the children who would lead England into the twentieth century.

GLOSSARY

aristocrats The most privileged members of the upper class, who inherited prestigious titles and large estates.

dioceses A diocese (pronounced *DIE-uh-seez*) is a large area made up of a number of parishes, under the administration of a bishop. At the end of the nineteenth century, there were thirty-seven Anglican dioceses in England and Wales.

Evangelical A form of Christianity whose followers believe that the Bible is the infallible word of God and who are dedicated to spreading the Gospel.

Gospel The message of love and salvation preached by Jesus Christ and his disciples. *Gospel* can also refer to the first four books of the New Testament, which tell the story of Christ's life and teachings.

High Church A formal, conservative faction within the Church of England, whose followers emphasize traditional Catholic elements in their worship services; also referred to as Anglo-Catholic.

Industrial Revolution The historical period marking the introduction of power-driven machinery and the social changes that resulted. The Industrial Revolution began in England in the mid- to late 1700s.

justices of the peace The chief authorities of a parish, who judged legal cases and tended to parish business such as organizing public works, dispensing public charity, and supervising workhouses. In 1888 much of the justices' power was transferred to elected county councils.

Low Church A faction within the Church of England whose followers do not use elaborate, highly structured rituals in their worship services, instead emphasizing the less formal Protestant traditions. Most Low Church Anglicans are Evangelical in their beliefs and practices.

parish The basic unit of local government. In the 1830s Great Britain was divided into some 15,000 parishes, ranging in size from a few clusters of country cottages to large city neighborhoods.

Parliament The national legislature of Great Britain.

propitiation A sacrifice or offering that turns away God's wrath. For Christians, Christ's death on the cross was the propitiation that regained God's favor for humankind.

Protestant Reformation A sixteenth-century religious movement that began with attempts to reform the Roman Catholic Church and resulted in the establishment of a number of Protestant churches.

Sabbatarianism The strict observance of the Sabbath.

squire A term of courtesy commonly used for a man of the gentry class whose family had lived in a country community for many generations. The gentry ranked below the aristocrats, and they inherited land but not titles.

tithe An annual tax collected in each parish to support the local Anglican church and clergyman.

FOR FURTHER READING

Ashby, Ruth. *Victorian England*. New York: Marshall Cavendish, 2003.

Damon, Duane C. *Life in Victorian England*. New York: Thomson Gale, 2006.

Mitchell, Sally. *Daily Life in Victorian England*. Westport, CT: Greenwood Press, 1996.

Pool, Daniel. *What Jane Austen Ate and Charles Dickens Knew*. New York: Simon and Schuster, 1993.

Swisher, Clarice. *Victorian England*. San Diego, CA: Lucent Books, 2001.

Wilson, Laura. *Daily Life in a Victorian House*. New York: Puffin Books, 1993.

ONLINE INFORMATION

Anglican Timeline: 1833-1890, The Victorian Era. Ed Friedlander, Society of Archbishop Justus, 2000.
http://justus.anglican.org/resources/timeline/

BBC Religion and Ethics: Church of England. British Broadcasting Corporation, 2009.
www.bbc.co.uk/religion/religions/christianity/cofe/

History in Focus: The Victorian Era. Institute of Historical Research, 2001.
www.history.ac.uk/ihr/Focus/Victorians/

Life in Victorian England. Copyright 1999-2009 Excelsior Information Systems Limited.
www.aboutbritain.com/articles/life-in-victorian-england.asp

Who Were the Victorians? Mandy Barrows, Woodlands Junior School, Tonbridge, Kent, England, 2008.
www.woodlands-junior.kent.sch.uk/Homework/victorians.html

SELECTED BIBLIOGRAPHY

Altick, Richard D. *Victorian People and Ideas*. New York: W. W. Norton, 1973.

Arnstein, Walter L. *Britain Yesterday and Today: 1830 to the Present*. 8th ed. Boston: Houghton Mifflin, 2001.

Avery, Gillian. *Victorian People in Life and in Literature*. New York: Holt, Rinehart, and Winston, 1970.

Clark, G. Kitson. *The Making of Victorian England*. Cambridge, MA: Harvard University Press, 1963.

Dyos, H. J., and Michael Wolff, eds. *The Victorian City: Images and Realities*. Vol. 2. London: Routledge and Kegan Paul, 1973.

Flanders, Judith. *Inside the Victorian Home: A Portrait of Domestic Life in Victorian England*. New York: W. W. Norton, 2004.

Horn, Pamela. *Labouring Life in the Victorian Countryside*. Abingdon, Oxon, England: Alan Sutton, 1995.

Mingay, G. E. *Rural Life in Victorian England*. Stroud, Gloucestershire, England: Sutton Publishing, 1998.

Moore, James R., ed. *Religion in Victorian Britain*. Vol. 3: *Sources*. Manchester, England: Manchester University Press, 1991.

Paterson, Michael. *Voices from Dickens' London*. Cincinnati, OH: David & Charles, 2006.

Picard, Liza. *Victorian London: The Life of a City, 1840-1870*. New York: St. Martin's, 2005.

Pike, E. Royston. *"Golden Times": Human Documents of the Victorian Age*. New York: Frederick A. Praeger, 1967.

Souden, David. *The Victorian Village*. London: Collins and Brown, 1991.

Thompson, Flora. *Lark Rise to Candleford*. Harmondsworth, Middlesex, England: Penguin Books, 1974.

Tucker, Herbert F., ed. *A Companion to Victorian Literature and Culture*. Malden, MA: Blackwell, 1999.

Ward, Sadie. *Seasons of Change: Rural Life in Victorian and Edwardian England*. London: George Allen and Unwin, 1982.

SOURCES FOR QUOTATIONS

ABOUT VICTORIAN ENGLAND

p. 6 "Since it has pleased": Queen Victoria, *Queen Victoria in Her Letters and Journals*, edited by Christopher Hibbert (New York: Viking, 1985), p. 23.

p. 7 "an age of transition": Sir Henry Holland, "The Progress and Spirit of Physical Science," *Edinburgh Review*, July 1858; quoted at www.archive.org/stream/essaysonscientif00hollrich/essaysonscientif00hollrich_djvu.txt

CHAPTER 1: A CHRISTIAN NATION

p. 9 "Religious life": Brooke Herford, *A Protestant Poor Friar: The Life-Story of Travers Madge* (Boston: Damrell and Upham, 1892; first published 1867), p. 137.

p. 11 "immense importance": Queen Victoria to Archbishop Benson, January 3, 1890; quoted in Walter Walsh, *The Religious Life and Influence of Queen Victoria* (Whitefish, MT: Kessinger Publishing, 2005; first published 1902), p. 261.

p. 12 "such a scene": Lord Shaftesbury, describing a service at St. Alban's Church in London in 1866; quoted in Picard, *Victorian London*, pp. 286-287.

p. 15 "rise as early": Thomas Wright, *Some Habits and Customs of the Working Classes, Written by a Journeyman Engineer* (1867); quoted in Pike, *"Golden Times,"* pp. 267-268.

p. 15 "nine out of ten": Thompson, *Lark Rise to Candleford*, p. 209.

p. 16 "the so-called Church": Edmund Gosse, *Father and Son: A Study of Two Temperaments* (1907); at http://www.fullbooks.com/Father-and-Son2.html

p. 16 "on the true faith": From the Oath of Allegiance taken by members of Parliament; the phrase was eliminated in the Parliamentary Oaths Act of 1886.

p. 16 "degenerate children": the Bishop of Cashel, April 27, 1858; quoted in Moore, *Religion in Victorian Britain*, pp. 497, 498.

CHAPTER 2: STONE CHURCHES AND SOARING CATHEDRALS

p. 19 "I went into the churchyard": *Kilvert's Diary, 1870-1879: Selections from the Diary of the Rev. Francis Kilvert*, edited by William Plomer. (Norwich, England: Fletcher and Son, 1964), p. 119.

p. 20 "These sittings": Horace Mann, *Census of Great Britain, 1851: Religious Worship in England and Wales*, abridged ed. (London: George Routledge, 1854), p. 83.

p. 20 "Whereas in 1801": ibid., p. 75.

p. 22 "One chief cause": ibid., p. 94.

p. 25 "a tiny place": Thompson, *Lark Rise to Candleford*, pp. 209-210.

CHAPTER 3: THE MEN OF THE CHURCHES AND CHAPELS

p. 27 "Usually the clergyman": P. Anderson Graham, *The Rural Exodus: The Problem of the Village and the Town* (London: Methuen and Co., 1892), p. 51.

p. 30 "prudent people": *The Position of the Agricultural Labourer in the Past and in the Future* (London: W. Reeves, 1885); quoted in Avery, *Victorian People*, pp. 156-157.

p. 30 "great and visible change": The Reverend G. A. Selwyn, *The Work of Christ in the World* (Cambridge: n.p., 1855); quoted in Clark, *The Making of Victorian England*, p. 153.

p. 31 "The vicar's innovations": Richard Jefferies, *Hodge and His Masters* (Charleston, SC: BiblioBazaar, 2006; originally published 1880), pp. 191, 194-195.

p. 33 "the cultivation and exercise": the Reverend John Cale Miller, rector of St. Martin's Church, Birmingham, 1846-1866; quoted in Dyos and Wolff, *The Victorian City*, p. 831.

p. 33 "Instead of dining": P. Anderson Graham, *The Rural Exodus: The Problem of the Village and the Town* (London: Methuen and Co., 1892), p. 52.

p. 35 "having the poor people": "Clergy Visitation Returns for Oxford Diocese for 1860," at Bodleian Library, Oxford University, England; quoted in Horn, *Labouring Life in the Victorian Countryside*, p. 166.

CHAPTER 4: WIVES AND CHILDREN

p. 37 "The distinguishing characteristics": Anonymous, *Hints to a Clergyman's Wife; or, Female Parochial Duties Practically Illustrated*, 2nd ed. (London: Samuel Holdsworth, 1838); quoted in Moore, *Religion in Victorian Britain*, p. 245.

p. 38 "private . . . walks": ibid., pp. 245-247.

p. 42 "reciting from memory": Thompson, *Lark Rise to Candleford*, p. 179.

p. 42 "an enormous Bible": M. Vivian Hughes, *A London Girl of the Eighties* (London: Oxford University Press, 1936); quoted in Flanders, *Inside the Victorian Home*, pp. 85-86.

p. 43: "Matins in the morning": *Within Living Memory*, Norfolk Federation of Women's Institutes, 1971; quoted in Horn, *Labouring Life in the Victorian Countryside*, p. 173.

p. 43 "the state of mind": *Mr. J. Edward White's Report on the Metal Manufacturers of the Birmingham District*, Children's Employment Commission, 3rd report (1864); quoted in Pike, *"Golden Times,"* p. 125.

p. 45 "'Oh!' she cried": Hesba Stretton (Sarah Smith), *Jessica's First Prayer* (1867); at http://www3.shropshire-cc.gov.uk/etexts/E000286.htm

CHAPTER 5: CELEBRATING THE FAITH

p. 47 "Every Sunday": Thompson, *Lark Rise to Candleford*, p. 209.

p. 48 "Sunday in London": Hippolyte Taine, *Notes on England*, translated by W. F. Rae (London: W. Isbister, 1874), p. 9.

p. 48 "remember the Sabbath day": Exodus 20:8 (New Revised Standard Version).

p. 48 "there were many things": Gwen Raverat, *Period Piece: A Victorian Childhood* (Bath, England: Clear Press, 2003; first published 1952), p. 102.

p. 50 "sang in the choir": S. J. Tyrell, *A Countryman's Tale* (London: Constable, 1973); quoted in Horn, *Labouring Life in the Victorian Countryside*, p. 171.

p. 50 "everlasting" and "would hammer away": Thompson, *Lark Rise to Candleford*, p. 211.

p. 51 "We came down to breakfast": Edmund Gosse, *Father and Son* (London: Penguin Books, 1989; first published 1907), pp. 194-195.

p. 52 "mild sins" and "one-sided conversations": Thompson, *Lark Rise to Candleford*, pp. 216, 217.

p. 52 "with the whole family": ibid., p. 215.

p. 54 "We have had numbers": William Tayler, diary, December 26, 1837; quoted in John Burnett, ed., *Useful Toil: Autobiographies of Working People from the 1820s to the 1920s* (London: Routledge, 1994), pp. 182-183.

CHAPTER 6: FROM CRADLE TO GRAVE

p. 57 "The sun was shining": Frances Hodgson Burnett, *The One I Knew the Best of All: A Memory of the Mind of a Child* (New York: Charles Scribner's Sons, 1893), pp. 152-153.

p. 60 "The mind reverts": the Reverend Benjamin John Armstrong, diary, February 7, 1854; quoted in Flanders, *Inside the Victorian Home*, p. 237.

p. 61 "You will let": Thomas Charles Geldart, master of Trinity Hall, Cambridge; quoted in Avery, *Victorian People*, p. 146.

p. 62 "The funeral was": Jeannette Marshall; quoted in Flanders, *Inside the Victorian Home*, p. 373.

p. 63 "The Various Periods": A Member of the Aristocracy, *Manners and Rules of Good Society; or, Solecisms to be Avoided*, 35th ed. (London: Frederick Warne and Co., 1913), pp. 242-246.

CHAPTER 7: A CRISIS OF FAITH

p. 65 "There is not a creed": Matthew Arnold, "The Study of Poetry"; in General Introduction to *The English Poets*, edited by Thomas Humphry Ward, vol. 1 (London: Macmillan and Co., 1880), p. xvii.

p. 68 "If only the Geologists": John Ruskin, private letter, 1851; quoted in George Allan Cate, ed., *The Correspondence of Thomas Carlyle and John Ruskin* (Stanford, CA: Stanford University Press, 1982), p. 14.

p. 70 "In the future": Charles Darwin, *On the Origin of Species by Means of Natural Selection, or the Preservation of Favored Races in the Struggle for Life* (New York: D. Appleton and Co., 1878; first published 1859), pp. 428-429.

p. 71 "speculations" and "moral and spiritual": Samuel Wilberforce, *On Darwin's "Origin of Species"* (1860); at www.fordham.edu/halsall/mod/1860wilberforce-darwin.html

p. 71 "The Origin of Species": Thomas H. Huxley, *On Species and Races, and Their Origin* (1860); quoted in Moore, *Religion in Great Britain*, p. 416.

p. 72 "reverence is the handmaid": ibid.

INDEX

ABOUT THE AUTHOR

VIRGINIA SCHOMP wrote her first short story (starring a magical toad) in kindergarten. She spent the rest of her school years with her nose in a book, pulling it out just long enough to earn a Bachelor of Arts degree in English Literature at Penn State University. Following graduation, she worked at several different publishing companies, learning about the day-to-day details of writing and producing books. After fifteen years of helping other writers realize their dreams, she decided that it was time to become a published writer herself. Since then she has written more than seventy books for young readers on topics including dinosaurs, dolphins, occupations, American history, ancient cultures, and ancient myths. Ms. Schomp lives in the Catskill Mountain region of New York, where she enjoys hiking, gardening, watching old movies on TV and new anime online, and, of course, reading, reading, and reading.